THE PUT-ON

modern fooling and modern mistrust

Jacob Brackman

Illustrated by Sam Kirson

Designed by Douglas Benezra

HENRY REGNERY COMPANY · CHICAGO

Excerpt from "Apologia" appeared *Ramparts Magazine,*
February 1967. Copyright © 1967 by *Ramparts Magazine*
and reprinted with permission.

Except for the Introduction, text by Jacob Brackman
originally published in *The New Yorker* in slightly
different form.

Text copyright © 1967, 1971 by Jacob Brackman
Art copyright © 1971 by Sam Kirson and Douglas Benezra

Photo of Bob Dylan by Charles Gatewood
Art on pages iv, v, 21-24, 94-99, 114-119
photographed by Robert Hoebermann

Published by Henry Regnery Company
114 West Illinois Street, Chicago, Illinois 60610
Manufactured in the United States of America
Library of Congress Catalog Card Number: 73-143847

To my mother and father, right?

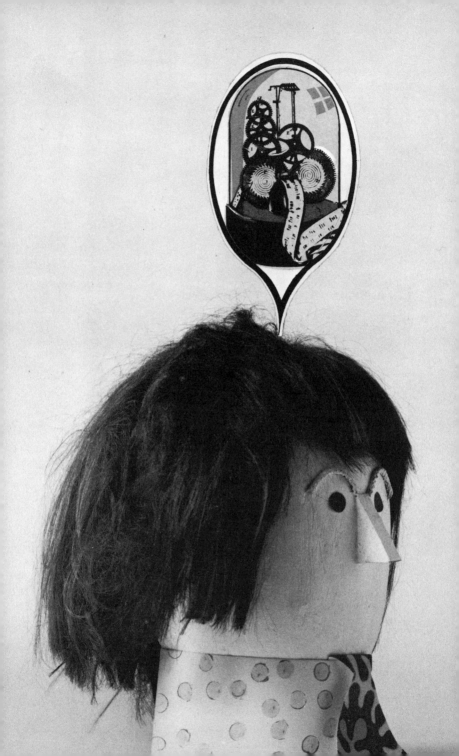

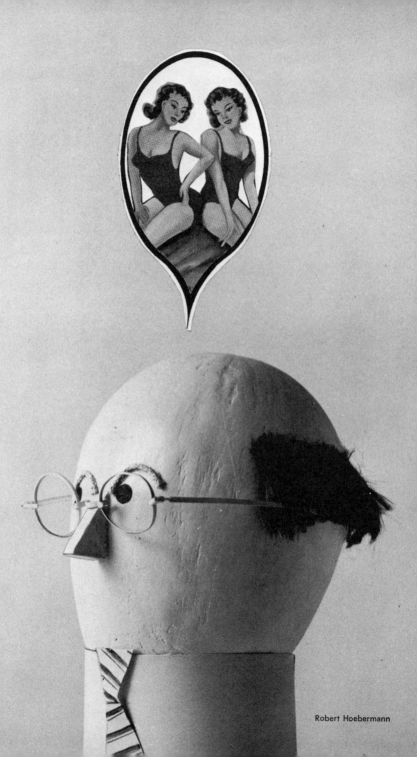

Robert Hoebermann

INTRODUCTION

Along with some others, and a bit in advance of lots more, I went through a period of intense preoccupation with the Dallas assassination mysteries. Of course, I'd been tricked about public events before—the U-2, the Bay of Pigs, our Vietnam "Advisors," the Dominican Intervention, the freedom of Blacks, the dangers of pot—but during this period, which peaked several months before the third anniversary of Jack Kennedy's murder, it was as if all the times I'd been deceived, as an American, had come to focus on this single most bald and crucial deception. For a time, there seemed to be a symbolic imperative: to learn how and why They had arranged to get the President, and to learn who They were.

From the beginning of 1966 until the middle of 1967 I spent occasional (but exhaustingly concentrated) weeks with Dick Gregory, who was then carrying a satchel full of supersuspicious assassination "evidence." I vastly admire Gregory. During those eighteen months, I arrogated his apocalyptic vision of American life. (He demanded that I grow a moustache. Moustaches were to be the signal for sparing particular whites when sniper fire began flashing from city windows. I could rarely tell for sure when Gregory was "jes playin." In any case, I grew the moustache. Let's just say to be on the safe side. An uncanny proportion of Gregory's riffs seemed to occupy a wide, uncharted territory between "playin" and the deadly earnest. People who chose to take him simply one way or the other were always missing out on the richness of his metaphor. There was no profit, I found, in trying to explicate his parables. Those who had ears to hear, heard).

Exactly whom Gregory seemed ever on the verge of accusing never became altogether clear to me. But there could be no doubt that he inclined to a Grand Conspiracy view of events. Often, it sounded as if no government hotshot would escape incrimination by the time he was done.

Another friend whom I revered, on almost completely different grounds, as ardently as I did Gregory, argued with me cogently *against* the notion of a Grand Conspiracy. Allard Lowenstein (who won election to Congress a couple of years later) knew some of the prestigious gentlemen who sat on the Warren Commission, and knew Bobby, and knew others whom, he insisted, *could not* be covering up. Yet even Al admitted the possibility of a petty conspiracy—no people in high places, ergo no political consequences— with a larger, post-facto conspiracy to cover up investigational bungling.

By the time "Inquest, Rush to Judgment" and other books which challenged the Warren Commission's proceedings and conclusions were published, a kind of soberly hysterical obsession with the evidence had begun to break over the national media. Soon it appeared that the general populace was embracing a Gregorian conception of history. (At one point, a Gallup poll reported that 65% of Americans disbelieved the Warren Report.) Meanwhile, I myself was swerving toward the Lowensteinian position. Not that I ever bought the lone, mad Commie hypothesis; I just started feeling out of control, unreasonable. To tell the truth, I simply had no more opinions. No more guesses about what might have happened in Dallas.

Nevertheless, in the summer of 1966, I wrote (with Faye Levine) a spoof assassination review. To my surprise, it was published in the Assassination Anniversary issue of *Ramparts*, November 1966, which had a color photograph of John Kennedy on the cover, broken up like a jigsaw puzzle with missing pieces, and which contained several seriously incredible articles (documentation of violent deaths allegedly connected to Nov. 23, 1963, etc.) Three months later, *Ramparts'* editors printed the following "Apologia":

There is a best seller that isn't in print and that nobody can buy, and we suppose we are to blame: *Time of Assassins* by Ulov G. K. Leboeuf. Levittown, N.Y.: Ulov G. K. Leboeuf. 4 Vols. I: 495 pp., II: 387 pp., III: 697 pp., IV: 460 pp. $24. It is, in case you haven't guessed, a phony, reviewed in a satirical review of Warren Commission books in the November RAMPARTS. (See also Letters, p. 5.) We thought the satire obvious,

3

but we have been wrong before and booksellers across the country have been besieged with orders for Leboeuf. Although sorry about all that, we are restraining the market society urge to talk to a ghostwriter friend about whipping out something to fill the demand.

Though the Leboeuf caper gave RAMPARTS an embarrassed moment or two, things, ladies, were worse at the Boston Globe. Two Globe ace reporters went out of their way to dismiss many of the Warren Commission critics, including and especially RAMPARTS as irresponsible and unbelievable. Then the authors postulated that the Commission should be reopened anyway, because despite these crackpots, what they considered substantive questions had been raised in really serious works about the assassination, among which, the Globe reported, was the study of Ulov G. K. Leboeuf of Levittown . . .

I should point out here that the Boston *Globe,* contrary to *Ramparts'* declaration, discussed Leboeuf as a "critic of undetermined reliability." A small fact, and far removed from the big issues —but a fact, bygod! Before long, very little about *l'affaire Leboeuf* remained at all clear to me. I did not know what to make of so many people taking the piece seriously. It had gone so far as to postulate five American Intelligence agents, sent to Dallas two years and six months before the assassination, "to live with Lee Harvey Oswald precisely to learn to be replicas of him." Soon the review, like a mechanical doll gone quietly haywire, was pointing the accusatory finger in every direction:

At various times during the years in which the maneuvers were incubating, the help of different political groups was enlisted: sometimes the Castroites, sometimes the anti-Castroites, sometimes the Communist-anarchists, and sometimes the radical right. Leboeuf presents convincing new evidence linking a number of prominent millionaire conservatives, as well as a few beer, oil, and birth control trusts, with the plot. The case for an inside job is persuasive, if not incontrovertible.

Leboeuf shows, for instance, that the angle of the bullet hole in Kennedy's back, heretofore a subject of vigorous dispute, is of less significance than the fact, revealed by the Tupferman silicone test on the plastic seatcovers of the Presidential automobile, that the bullet was fired less than .0002 of a millisecond before making contact with the target within the car. This means that however fast the bullet might have been travelling, from either the grassy knoll or the book depository, it still would not have been able to reach the car so rapidly. The conclusion is startling: the Kennedy bullet must have been fired either from within the car itself or from extreme proximity to it.

It went on like that. People disbelieved the findings of seven eminent statesmen, and took it seriously. I soon came to suspect that some of them knew something I didn't. Even the letters congratulating our courage ("Glad to have you catching white hot rivets in the same league. We all speak the language of dialectics. . . . It's tough and big so hold on to your bulletproof vest . . .") began to unnerve me. Had I inadvertently worried the true conspirators? Was I therefore now a marked man? (We non-believers can transgress the commandments freely; but we're still prey to occasional ripples of panic at punishment in store on the off chance He *does* exist.)

One great source of confusion was the inaccessibility of familiar categories in which to consider the Leboeuf "spoof." Originally, it was to be a parody of a *New York Review* review of Lane, Epstein, et al. by Richard Popkin, in which he first advanced his "second Oswald" theory. Then, because this review seemed too slight and obscure to support a parody, I thought of parodying apocalyptic assassination literature in general. We'd soberly "review" a patently insane book. However, some peculiar things happened in the writing.

The first was that parody—of literary style, of wild speculation masquerading as syllogism— got mixed up with satire—of actual political events. The second was that I found myself sprinkling stuff I knew, or suspected, to be true (including "facts" I'd heard from Gregory) among preposterous falsehoods. The third was that my own tentative and contradictory feelings about what constituted good or bad taste rather obscured who and what I was making fun of. Was it reviewers who swallowed nonsense whole? Believers of the Warren Report? The buffs? (Leboeufs?) The blind extremes of the controversy itself? The very question of "taste?"

When the letters started coming in, I was doubly confused about how to respond to the way people responded. Sitting down to answer earnest requests for further information, I couldn't settle

6

on the proper tone in which to break the news. Some people said that they'd been fooled and enjoyed it immensely, some that they'd been fooled and outraged, some that they hadn't been fooled for a second, and screw off. (We hadn't intended to "fool" anybody.) Edward Jay Epstein said it was one of the funniest things he'd ever read. Sylvia Meagher called it "intellectual and moral gangrene," "a gratuitous and vicious attack on every researcher and critic of the Warren Report." I couldn't figure out whether or not to be ashamed of it.

It did seem, though, that some complex failures of conception and courage had made it something different from a hoax, or a legitimate parody or satire; it was not irony, it was not joshing or kidding—it was something else. It had to do with a new kind of "sophistication" that capitalized on our confusion, and that brought the cynical, aggressive elements of wit perilously close to the surface. Whatever it was, I realized that it had been happening a lot lately: in conversation, art, politics, fashion.

There was some question about whether to "update" the essay, which was written end of 1966-beginning 1967. I remember then—I was in Martinique, recouping some psychic losses sustained during an abortive Ph.D. candidacy—trying to long-distance voodoo *The New Yorker* into publishing it quickly. I found the inevitable delay between its private completion and public appearance driving me a bit up the wall.

After I'd spent a couple of months considering put-ons—how they worked, what was behind them, what they might mean about contemporary sensibility—new examples, new twists to theories would suggest themselves daily, demanding revision or more writing. I very much wanted to close the thing out on my own books. Like most of my work thus far, it had already gotten out of hand; I was wasting time and attention on it. Furthermore, a few smart critics were already sort of talking about put-ons (I recall Albert Goldman on "Candy," Walter Kerr on "Mac-Bird," Renata Adler on "Modesty Blaise"). We all sensed it was there, but no one had quite refined the vocabulary to get at it quite. The phenomenon quickly seemed to me so ubiquitous, and everyone's latent consciousness of it so over-ripe, that I imagined another account (saturated with misapprehensions, of course) would roll off the presses somewhere at any moment.

That would have been bad only incidentally because, not believing that I could necessarily lay it out prettiest, I wished to do so first. The main problem was that once something so close to the surface, and yet not quite arrived at the surface, gets publicly "explained," then self-consciousness

8

begins turning back in upon itself in a kind of spiral, and everything shifts.

Susan Sontag's famous numbered essay, "Notes on Camp," illustrates that centrifugal movement. Miss Sontag was not the first to notice "camp," but once she had written about it, another critic could not come along and pretend she hadn't. This has almost nothing to do with proprietorship of an idea, but rather with what happens to an idea when it moves from the classy preconscious into the popular consciousness. Her disjunct essay in *Partisan Review* was read by tens of thousands, but its reverberations affected the culture consumed by hundreds of millions. Eventually, of course, the outer circles of reverberation had little to do with Miss Sontag's sense; one could, if one cared to, argue that they'd have happened without her, as one could that x, y or z would have happened without the Beatles.

What has been, really, an outlaw form was rapidly institutionalized. Whereas Miss Sontag had been describing a method of appreciation, her rules were embraced as principles of manufacture. People who had been connoisseurs of camp prior to its public articulation dropped it like a hot potato; their ranks were overreplenished with ignorant hoardes from Hollywood, Madison Avenue and Womrath, U.S.A., hungry for respectable culture that required of them neither erudition nor discrimination. This is the baldest simplification, of course. But if you wanted to write about camp after Miss Sontag did,

9

you could do a fun popularization (as Gloria Steinem did for *Life*) or, more demandingly, you could trace how the experience of camp expanded and degnerated, as more people became more imprecisely aware of what it was about.

Updating. If "updating" this essay were to mean exchanging more current jokes and performers for ones since disappeared, and impending how there came to be "put-on" head boutiques, and TV game shows, and a Sears Put-On clothing shop, and publishers crowing "This is the novel that makes you ask: *Is the author putting me on?*," and thousands of winkful commercials that seemed to say, "I know that you know that I'm trying to sell you. Let's you and me both goof on the product together."—if I were to "update" along these lines, and if I were to add little exegeses of Tiny Tim's wedding, Bob Downy's movies, Paul McCartney's death, then the piece would begin to stink of inauthenticity.

Cultural history now, for the first time ever, outstrips political-military history. Compare the pace of change in music, cinema, fashion and religion, 1966-1970, with that in government, labor, civil rights, Vietnam, or in indigenous Resistance. Yet who would think of "updating" an analysis of American politics written then: before McCarthy, before Johnson retired, before Robert Kennedy and Martin King were shot, before the Chicago Convention, and on and on. Either writing is worth looking at some years later, again or for the first time, or it must disappear. It does no

10

good to stretch it out across a larger expanse of time than its fibres will bear, to say, "It's as true today as it was then; ever as fresh as tomorrow's headlines."

I think you must let a piece like this stand—not in its syntax, necessarily, but within the limits of its original awareness—as a fragment of cultural history. It may have been valid to the precise present for a matter of months, or days; who will quibble now that time is so short? Once the vision's devoured, mulched and incorporated, unless it has been frozen somewhere, its moment—when only so much had happened, when only so much had been revealed—is lost forever. All we have left are "updated" reports, grotesquely stretched, debased and freshened up, as what played itself out between haircuts is made to seem the rage of a decade. If I were to do this piece today (which would itself be impossible) hardly anything in it would stay the same. Of things in the real world about which one can try to write, sensibility may be the slipperiest. If I won't write the new piece now, how can I go back and meddle with the old one?

I guess my fascination with the possibly fraudulent—with coming on and taking in; with being faked out; with the themes of deception, confusion and resentment—run back through my life, back to my earliest memories. So, for me, there's something constant about the material here, underneath the ephemera, most of it already gone and lost. Nevertheless, its elusiveness is most striking—our politics, our culture, our mood have gone through unforeseeably heavy changes—and that larger elusiveness is underscored for me by private resonances. All the friends this piece brings to mind, however attached to them I remain, have somehow faded from my life: Gregory and Lowenstein and Stanley Cavell, who were, at some curious remove, its inspiration; and several others who sat around with me then and helped think it through: Paul Lee, Paul Warshow, Faye Levine, Jack Kroll and, transcendently, William Shawn.

—Jacob Brackman
January, 1971

THE PUT-ON

modern fooling and modern mistrust

Patrons at a Pop gallery chuckle knowingly over a Roy Lichtenstein painting. A bearded young man at a party introduces himself as an undercover agent for the Green Berets. Senator Everett Dirksen recites a deep-throated, eye-rolling, super-rhetorical piece of bombast on God, Country, and Marigolds. Stokely Carmichael answers an interviewer who wants to know what must be done about Harlem: "Burn it to the ground and send one million black men up to invade Scarsdale." Oedipa Maas, wife of disc jockey Mucho Maas and patient of berserk psychiatrist Dr. Hilarius, is at last on the verge of unravelling the prodigious mystery of the Tristero syndicate on page 183 of Thomas Pynchon's much heralded second novel; there is no page 184. Representative Frank Thompson, of New Jersey, before a full session of Congress, proposes the Banana and Other Odd Fruit Disclosure and Reporting Act of 1967 to halt "the sinister spread" of "hallucinogenic" banana-peel smoking. A top-box-office spy film concludes, after a huge explosion wipes out secret agents from five countries (as well as French Legionnaires, United States Cavalrymen, and a Frugging battalion of Indian parachutists), with a mass ascent to Heaven.

15

Students opposed to the war in Vietnam arrive to testify at House Un-American Activities Committee hearings in bizarre costumes: one wears a Revolutionary War uniform, complete with tricorne hat; another identifies himself as James Bond; a third addresses the Chairman, Congressman Joseph Pool, of Texas, as Jo-Jo while under oath. Adam Clayton Powell summons newsmen to his Bimini hideaway for a big scoop; then he plugs his new record, "Keep the Faith, Baby." "What's the big story?" a reporter asks. "You've heard it, baby," Powell replies. The Beatles answer every question at a press conference by saying "Woof, woof." Someone asks if "Yellow Submarine" is a drug song, and Paul McCartney replies, "You have a dirty mind." In Mont-Saint-Michel, a pretty girl in leotards flourishes a trumpet, elaborately preparing for a street concert. Finally, she begins to blow horrible noises. Obviously, she can't play the trumpet at all. She passes a hat and people give her money. "WHAT DOES IT MEAN?—WHO KNOWS?" asks a *Times* headline above a rave review of "Gorilla Queen," in which a chorus line of apes sings the Chorale from Beethoven's Ninth and both a jungle girl and a blond to-be-sacrificed virgin seem to be men. The playwright's previous works include "Tarzan of the Flicks," "Indira Gandhi's Daring Device," and "The Life of Lady Godiva." Twiggy (31-22-32), the world's No. 1 model and London's "Girl of the Year," has thatched male hair, stands five feet six, weighs ninety-one pounds, wears short pants, sucks her finger, pouts, and answers reporters' questions with "I dunno." She is seventeen years old and earns a hundred and twenty dollars an hour. A famous artist is commissioned to paint the portrait of, say, Mrs. Felice Worthingham. "I'm very busy," he mutters. "Let's see . . ." He writes the words "Portrait of Mrs. Felice Worthingham" on a grubby torn-off piece of paper. Then he signs the jotting and hands it over to Mr. Worthingham, who has the "portrait" framed and pays the artist's usual fee—five thousand dollars. Man, you know *some*body's leg is being pulled. Or at least you think *maybe* it is.

By means of a subtle transformation in the ways artists deal with their audiences and people with one another, we suddenly have reason to distrust a good deal of art, fashion, and conversation—to withhold a flat-footed, honest response. More and more often, we suspect we are being tricked. What was once an occasional surprise tactic—called "joshing" around the turn of the century and "kidding" since the twenties—has been refined into the very basis of a new mode of communication. In all its permutations, this phenomenon is known as the "put-on." It occupies a fuzzy territory between simple leg-pulling and elaborate practical joke, between pointed lampoon and free-floating spoof.

Though there are suddenly many more of them, conversational put-ons are related to old-fashioned joshing and kidding, or to the sort of joke that Southerners call "funning" and Englishmen call "taking a mickey out of" someone. Not unlike the put-on, these older cousins depend upon a certain gullibility in the victim. They are like April-fool gags, perpetrated deadpan to get the victim to believe something that isn't so. Miniature hoaxes, their raison d'être is the surprise revelation of truth ("I was only kidding" or "It was just a gag") and laughter at the fall guy's credulity. Naturally, there were, and still are, habitual kidders or practical jokers. But the object of kidding, as of hoaxing, is always manifest: to *pass off* untruth as truth just for the fun of it. Ideally, there's no doubt in anyone's mind. At first, the victim believes the false to be true, whereas the kidder knows the truth. Then, the gulling accomplished, the kidder lets the victim know he's been taken for a ride. This payoff is the kidder's goal. With kidding and other hoax-derived precedents, the perpetrator smooths the rug out, has you stand on it, and then suddenly yanks it out from under you.

The put-on is more like one of those irregularly moving platforms at an amusement park. The victim must constantly struggle to maintain his balance, constantly awkward, even (perhaps especially) when the floor *stops* moving for an instant; i.e., a "straight" moment, which makes the victim feel he has been paranoid. As he re-adjusts himself to this vision, the floor, so to speak, starts moving again. If conversation with a kidder is spiced by bosh, conversation with a put-on artist is a process of escalating confusion and distrust. He doesn't deal in isolated little tricks; rather, he has developed a pervasive style of relating to others that perpetually casts what he says into doubt. The put-on is an *open-end* form. That is to say, it is rarely climaxed by having the "truth" set straight—when a truth, indeed, exists. "Straight" discussion, when one of the participants is putting the others on, is soon subverted and eventually sabotaged by uncertainty. His intentions, and his opinions, remain cloudy.

We remember the kidder as a good-natured, teasing sort—that moment when he rendered his victim absurd was quickly dissipated in the general laughter that followed. The put-on artist draws out that derisive moment; the gull has time to reflect (What's he up to? . . . He's trying to make a monkey out of me. . . . How should I respond?), and the joke's latent malice wells close to the surface. As the put-on pursues its

19

course (at times while the subject matter shifts), it becomes clear that the victim is the butt of a generalized ridicule. Occasionally, a victim will try to explain away his confusion by assuming that the put-on artist is "just being ironical"— that he really means precisely the reverse of everything he says. This interpretation is hardly more helpful than taking put-ons at face value. Irony properly suggests the *opposite* of what is explicitly stated, by means of peripheral clues— tone of voice, accompanying gestures, stylistic exaggeration, or previous familiarity with the ironist's real opinions. Thus, for "Brutus is an honorable man" we understand "Brutus is a traitor." Irony is unsuccessful when misunderstood. But the put-on, inherently, *cannot* be understood.

Irony: A known dove delivers an impassioned "kill the gooks" speech.

Put-on: Someone we don't know delivers the same hawk speech. It is wildly hyperbolical, and yet . . . Is he really a dove? Might he be caricaturing his own position? Might he be apolitical and arbitrarily lampooning one extreme? Might he be merely ridiculing the passion of the discussion? Does he know at all how he feels about the Vietnamese war? Does the confusion he produces in his audience mirror his own confusion? Does the put-on, his diversionary artillery, spare him the self-examination required for a "real stand"?

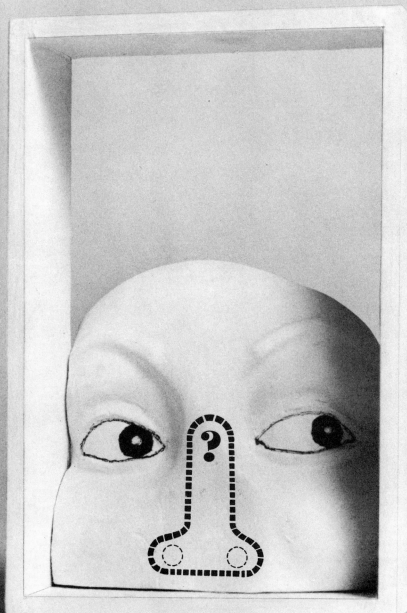

Robert Hoebermann

You put me on.

Robert Hoebermann

Robert Hoebermann

The deliberate ambiguities of conversational put-ons apply as well to put-ons in art, which are often mistaken for parodies or satires. Yet, according to long-established custom, the parody and the satire are rigorous, demanding forms, with the avowed and actual purpose of burlesquing preëxisting situations in art or life. A parody must imitate the original well, effectively exaggerating its peculiarities and weaknesses. In other words, to be good it must be sharp. It may be attacked for inadequate accuracy, pungency, or wit. The spoof (an old and annoying word now back in vogue for the vehicle of the put-on) need not be good to avert attack. It is too dangling, too slippery. It has only the *form* of satire, without the content, without the rules. It attacks, but from no real position of its own. Not holding any real position, it is itself invulnerable to attack.

When audiences "don't know how to take" a piece of work, it may now be the case that a highly ambiguous mode of presentation has rescued the artist from a head-on struggle with his material, from the most crucial dilemmas of art: What am I to make of my experiences? How do I feel about them? What do they teach me of the world? As conversational put-ons may disguise the fact that someone has nothing of interest to

25

say—may, indeed, give precisely the opposite impression—so have put-ons in art come to serve as a refuge for the untalented. This is not to suggest that gifted artists never affect the style of the put-on (the Beatles are excellent examples of artists who do) but, rather, that the style itself clogs critical judgment and scuttles aesthetic standards. The Intellectual Establishment, which once took a dim view of those who believed themselves so above art as to dissemble in its name, now seems eager to play pigeon to the put-on, and accepts—even welcomes—the implied abuse.

Admittedly, confusion or suspicion on the part of the Intellectual Establishment is historically a poor basis for mistrusting the intentions of artists. Almost every experimental or revolutionary artistic movement of the past—Romanticism, Impressionism, Symbolism, Surrealism, a dozen other isms—was in its time accused of being anti-art. Earnest Philistines of our century demanded to know whom Gertrude Stein and Ezra Pound thought they were fooling; they warned E. E. Cummings that he'd never put his nonsense verse over on readers. They exhorted Picasso that gallery-goers wouldn't be taken in by Cubism, and cried out when Jackson Pollock and Franz Kline tried to pass off random drippings and slashings as paintings. Schoenberg and Webern were believed to have carried sounds past the boundaries of music. Electronic composers were told that people had too much sense to be hoodwinked by "unmusical" cacophony.

Even as contemporary Goths ask, "Who are they trying to kid?," a new avant-garde public rises to testify that future sensibilities will vindicate Claes Oldenburg's proposed hamburger monument in Times Square, or Andy Warhol's eight-hour film of a sleeping man, or La Monte Young's ear-rending, interminable Drone. And perhaps they will. The debatable art of the current scene, as well as already exonerated cases from art history, underscore the crucial question of *intent*. We now believe that heretical movements of the past, doubted and maligned in their own time, were fostered by serious men who cared deeply about art, who struggled to liberate themselves from exhausted conventions in order to revitalize and restore its relevance. Aspects of these revolutions—the extravagances of Artaud-inspired theatre, or the Nihilistic underside of Dada, with its mustached Mona Lisas and empty canvases—we now consider wrong-headed, childish, chaotic, even destructive. But we are at the same time convinced that they were undertaken, whether in anger or fun, in good faith, with a profound commitment to art and its future.

Much "serious" art today—even seemingly outlandish art—is doubtless undertaken with the same commitment. The currency of the put-on, however, has given new meaning to recent Dadaist experimentation. Many art consumers, and some critics as well, have come to envisage contemporary art as a giant con game. The game is played in a spirit of desperate suspicion. Its ob-

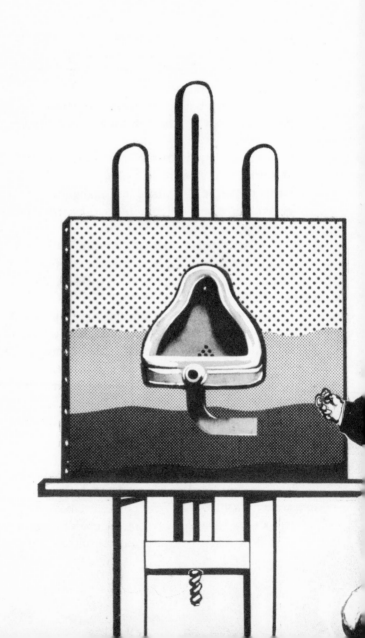

ject is twofold: to appreciate what is "good" and "real," and to avoid being taken in by the con jobs. A few modern critics—most notably, Marshall McLuhan—have tried to break up this game by, in effect, redefining art as anything you can put over on anybody. But the world of culture has too much at stake to accept any such permissive redefinition. Art critics, dealers, and curators must protect their identities (and jobs) as people of taste and discrimination. They must continue to insist that they *understand* what art is real and what art is phony, and that their judgment is fit to advise the public.

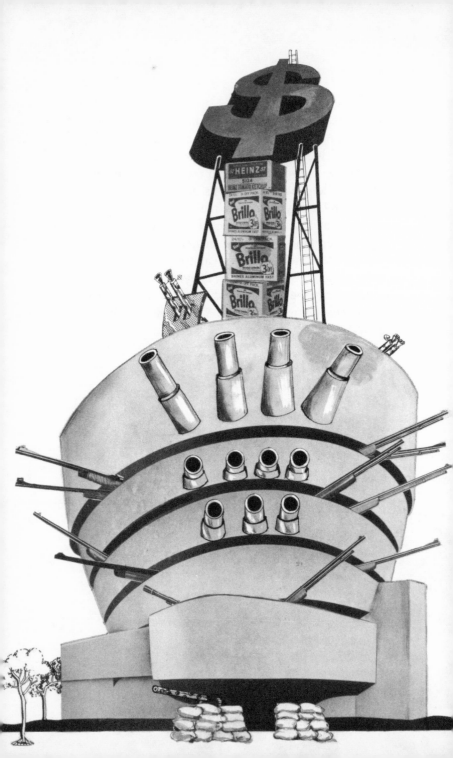

This staunch ortho-
doxy in the Cultural Establishment has several
peculiar results. A dangerously preëmptive sort
of subjectivism has taken over serious criticism.
For a critic to call work bad, he must often, in
the light of what he's already called good, tell us
that it is a fake. In other words, what he likes he
deems real art; what he doesn't like he deems
"anti-art," or put-on. Since the critic assumes his
job is to dope out the con game, disagreement
among critics becomes highly explosive. When
one considers bad something that others have
considered good, he is no longer simply challeng-
ing the merits of a specific work; he is telling the
public that his colleagues have been taken in by
fraud, that they are hoodwinked in their notions
of what constitutes art, that none of us really
knows for sure anymore what is real and good.
A terrible fear is thus generated throughout the
Cultural Establishment: in the galleries, the acad-
emies, the critical journals. Are we dismissing
genius? Are we elevating nonsense? Will someone
rock the boat? Will someone suddenly shout that
the Emperor is naked? Will someone simply come
along and *describe* the objects we have praised,
and will those objects then sound stupid?

One upshot of these fears is a wary, "sophisticated" tolerance toward new art—an intellectualized, jargon-full appreciation of it. Much of this art does, indeed, require tolerance, but tolerance of a far more relaxed sort. It is meant to "be experienced," to wash over an audience. Its put-ons are what may be called *set-breaking* put-ons. They afford one an opportunity to observe one's own consciousness reacting to "art" that contradicts all one's expectations of art. When a composer comes on-stage in a dinner jacket and seats himself at a grand piano, a familiar set is established. When he continues to sit there without playing a single note—when the audience realizes that his sitting there *is* the concert—the set is broken. There are perhaps three primary responses to a set-breaking aesthetic experience of this sort: (1) you leave; (2) you remain, listening to what other sounds are to be heard in the hall, examining how others in the audience respond to the "concert," and taking an inventory of your *own* responding consciousness; (3) you remain, trying to figure out whether the composer is "serious" or whether you, as a critical intelligence, are being conned. We know that everyone square leaves, or at least very badly wants to leave. Thus, tolerance—at galleries, concerts, Happenings, dance programs, independent cinema—has become a significant aspect of the contemporary aesthetic experience. Being able to bear put-ons has become one of the responsibilities of the modern audience.

32

The wrong kind of tolerance—suspicious endurance—has, furthermore, opened up the art scene to people who are able to capitalize on unacknowledged critical confusion. This sort of highly marketable wise-guy-ness, as opposed to seriously intended set-breaking, has made the put-on a fundamentally commercial form, finding its purest expression in television, Hollywood cinema, formula radio, fashion, Top Forty sound, advertising, and the most salable of popular art. Whereas artistic rebels of eras past embraced the most extreme risks in prosecuting their aesthetic ideas, popular artists can now *avoid* risk by the suggestion of a put-on. Possibly the bravest gamble a contemporary artist can take is to present himself as unequivocally serious, for he thereby risks making a fool of himself. This risk, along with the risk of appearing naïve, was once an inviolable prerogative of all creative work. Now we have come to believe that an artist who may be fooling cannot be a fool, and, conversely, that one who is in no way making fun of his own efforts is somehow humorless. It's open season on the unabashedly earnest. But as long as the artist's intentions are even slightly in doubt, most critics approach him with some caution.

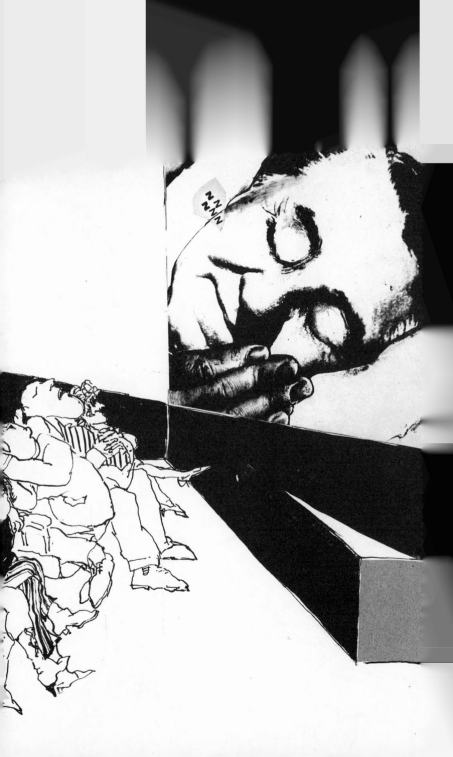

A put-on may be as short as a phrase or as long as a novel. Still more confounding, the purest put-ons are never altogether pure, never *unmistakable*. The put-on at once elevates the fraudulent and debases the true, rendering the entire proceedings questionable. A remark that *may be* a put-on casts a whole conversation into doubt; a few frames that may be a put-on make us wonder about a whole movie. The pervasive currency of the put-on generates an atmosphere charged with misplaced skepticism. Not even the painfully serious manage to escape incrimination. Is Marshall McLuhan just putting us on? Is John Cage? Is Norman Mailer, in "An American Dream"? Stan Brakhage, in "Dog Star Man"? Does Dwight Macdonald *really* like "MacBird" all that much? Can Frank Stella be laughing up his sleeve at the critical acclaim accorded his paintings? Richard Goldstein can't actually *believe* the Mamas and the Papas are as valid as Bach. Robert Rauschenberg must be kidding with some of those Happenings, right?

Curiously, this sort of misguided suspicion is tendered in a spirit of respect. (When a work is well reviewed nowadays, some critic is almost sure to inform us that the whole thing was a big joke, and so much the better.) If we like the art, jolly good show. If we don't, perhaps the artist is making fun of us. Perhaps we must give him credit for putting something over on us. If a piece of work is stupid, perhaps it's meant to show how stupid *we* are. Such notions are currently so ingrained as to somehow redeem art that is simply and honestly bad. In spite of his obvious ingenuousness, Andy Warhol is widely credited with pulling the wool over the public's eyes. Nothing of the kind. The public has shown itself ready to buy his meagre product, and he places it on the market as fast as his factories can turn it out. The people around Warhol, however—his co-manufacturers, and certain critics who know when to latch on to a good thing—have created an ambiguous, quasi-facetious aura about their work cult. So while Warhol remains true to his profoundly simplistic visions, consumers feel proud to participate in some vast joke on their peers, and on the very concept of beauty.

Time was when artistic hoax meant a talented unknown's offering his work under an opportune name to gain an audience. So Thomas Chatterton "discovered" "ancient" religious manuscripts and poems, Charles Vanderbourg the

49

poetry of "Clotilde," Prosper Mérimée the dramas of "Clara Gazul," Fritz Kreisler "lost compositions" of Vivaldi, Couperin, Popora, Pugnani, and Padre Martini. The works themselves were fine and deserving. Today, unknowns make names for themselves with hoax work. Even a painting chimpanzee has been employed to play this game. Talk circulates—"Is it for real?"—and the product sells.

Fascination with the possibly fraudulent, while a symptom of a New Sensibility, has powerful precedents in American culture. For a hundred years—from the Crédit Mobilier scandal and the Whiskey Ring fraud to Billie Sol Estes and Bobby Baker—a sizable number of Americans have been amused rather than enraged by the feats of audacity that gulled them. Such a climate enabled P. T. Barnum to become one of the prime architects of the Gilded Age. People took him to their hearts as the Prince of Humbug; they gave him license to deceive them. In a corrupt era, when the noblest impulses seemed to lead toward contempt and castigation of self and country, audiences implicitly demanded that they themselves be the butt of public jokes. When they laughed and applauded Barnum's unconvincing cozening, they symbolized the amused acquiescence of a republic duped by political sharks. Because his audience would accept bamboozlement as well as genuine spectacle, Barnum was at least partly relieved of responsibility for coming across with the real McCoy. "People like to be fooled," he's supposed to have said. "There's a sucker born every minute." Yet, despite exaggerated claims for his presentations, not *all* of them were frauds—and he drew the line between the sort of hokum that came to be known as Barnumism and the out-and-out swindle. (He emptied out his packed freak museum, for example, with a fancy sign that read, "This Way to the Egress." Customers eagerly went through the appointed door and found themselves in an alley.) So even his hip clientele could never be sure of an exhibit's authenticity: perhaps this Negro woman *was* more than a hundred and sixty years old, perhaps she *was* George Washington's nurse. They asked a question much in vogue today: "Is this for real?"

Barnum's "Greatest Show on Earth" anticipated the three classic elements of the put-on: the come-on (buildup, enticement), the fake-out (revelation or suspicion that things are not what they seem), and the cop-out (pulling the whole thing off without necessarily delivering the goods).

61

Let me define my terms. The come-on is like an introduction, only more elaborate. It is the gestaltic self-presentation. The fake-out is like a surprise only bigger. It is a radical contradiction of one's presuppositions. The fake-out unmasks the come-on. In combination, they yield the put-on—like a hoax, only smaller.

1. You're sucked in.
2. You become confused.
3. You resent (or appreciate) having been tricked.

The cop-out is like a fink-out, only more graceful. It is getting away with a renege. Here is a hypothetical model of the agglomerate phenomenon:

You go to the theatre to see a magician. He *comes on* like a magician, in tails and cape, and announces that for his first trick he will make a pigeon vanish into thin air. He conceals the bird under a kerchief, utters an incantation, and whisks the kerchief away. The pigeon is still there. He looks confused. You *are* confused. He tries again; again the disappearance fails. On the third try, titters run through the audience. On the fourth, the house is in stitches. You've been *faked out*. You have two options:

> (1) "Hey! What is this? I came to see a magician."
> (2) "Hey! Terrific! The guy's really a *comedian*. He had me going there for a minute."

The fake-out has transformed his come-on into a put-on.

Now, if this fellow had really been a magician he would have finked out, busted. Instead, he's a success—everybody's laughing. He's *copped out*.

After all, you paid admission to see a trick. Is the put-on a lower order of trick than a real disappearance? Is it easier? Cheaper? Or is it a double trick? If the pigeon had vanished, that would have been a trick *for* you. The revelation that the magician was not a magician has been

a trick *on* you—but if you enjoyed being fooled, of course, it's been for you as well. When the "magician" continues his act in the same vein of bungled abracadabra, we are dealing in straightforward comedy. Once the fake-out has been fully realized, the put-on, strictly speaking, is over. The purest put-ons commence credibly, plant their own seeds of doubt, promote growing confusion, and leave their victims foundering. The secret of maintaining a put-on, therefore, is protracting the fake-out.

The greatest fake-out protractor in modern literature, the absolute master of the extended put-on, is probably Grand Guy Grand, the multibillionaire hero of Terry Southern's "The Magic Christian." The purpose of all Grand's activity is "making it hot" for people—embarrassing or frustrating them beyond all bounds—and the book progresses through a series of immense practical jokes in which Grand expends vast sums putting on people he doesn't know. At one point, he purchases a movie theatre so that he can doctor the Hollywood features he shows by splicing in shocking or outlandish footage that he has had specially filmed. In the scene in "The Best Years of Our Lives" where the wounded war hero is talking quietly to his girl, there comes a split second when the audience— or part of the audience—suddenly sees one of the soldier's prosthetic hands slip under the girl's skirt. The climactic episode of the book concerns an exclusive, very expensive world cruise Grand organizes that methodically disintegrates into a nightmare for his captive passengers. (Strange men are seen attacking the captain on closed-circuit TV, the foghorn jams and blasts continuously, nothing but potatoes is left in the larder toward the end of the trip, and so on.) Jocko de Paris, the vicious military-academy hazer of Calder Willingham's "End as a Man," is the prince of put-on artists in a realistic context. Still fanciful, but stripped of humor, his put-ons appear to be the Devil's craft.

Willingham is a precursor and Southern a member of a fraternity of current writers sometimes lumped under the banner of Black Humor. They not only explore characters who embody the put-on but seem themselves bent on putting on an audience of liberal intellectuals, accustomed to the belief that life can be explained and understood. Borrowing from the self-mockery of Stendhal, from the super-parody of Joyce, Proust, and Kafka, they invent insane literary forms, send grotesque people with impossible names moving through mad worlds. They sprinkle their work with interruptions asking, in effect, "What does this stuff *mean*?," thereby ridiculing in advance an element of potential stupidity in what may be an altogether proper question. (We are supposed to have learned by now that one does not ask what art means.) An anything-goes spirit of apocalyptic laughter serves as a rationale for any extravagance and for the dramatization of brutal and regressive fantasies. ("Candy," a venomous narrative, was hailed as a tangy send-up of pornography.) Writers like Bruce Jay Friedman, Thomas Pynchon, and Joseph Heller seem to offer all-encompassing megacosms in which puzzling loose ends (frequently stunning in themselves) seem ever about to draw together and be clarified. Instead, problems are somehow sidestepped or reduced to banalities. More often than not, a joke is made of the whole business. As the stories seem teetering on the edge of an ultimate answer, they cop out by faking us out, leaving us in vague agitation, perhaps swindled out of an understanding that the author possessed but perversely withheld.

Are any of these writers dealing in outright put-ons? As with much of contemporary art, it is impossible to say for certain. Some prefer to keep their positions ambiguous with regard to intention, treating their work as mysteriously apart from conscious design. ("The critics say it's a brilliant joke? Well, maybe so. Maybe deep down I meant it that way. I'll trust my own unconscious.") This tack enables them to wait and see which way the critical winds blow before committing themselves. Others bravely resist such temptations. When one reviewer praised "Eternal Fire" as a parody, Calder Willingham (whose early collection, "Gates of Hell," unwittingly fathered many varieties of put-on style) insisted that his novel was absolutely serious. Occasionally, also, basically "straight" writers employ elements of the put-on—especially the fake-out—to achieve certain effects, unintentionally copping out on a difficult problem.

A distinctive sort of literary or cinematic fake-out hinges on the sudden demolition of a mood, usually high tragedy collapsing into bathos. ("A joke," Nietzsche said, "is the epitaph on an emotion.") Sometimes the fake-out works the other way around—as in the high-spirited scene from "Shoot the Piano Player" when a gun farcically drawn and twirled, Lone Ranger style, shoots the heroine dead—choking a laugh into a sputter of dismay. Such abrupt reversals produce confusion about the entire piece—"Is the whole thing just a joke?"—and condition audiences against allowing themselves to feel deeply about anything on the page or on the screen.

Another non-episodic variety of the extended put-on is commonly called "putting someone through changes." This technique—as old as Euripides—now lies at the heart of a suddenly ubiquitous entertainment mode, the spoof thriller, whether detective or spy. Watching imbroglios riddled with quadruple crosses or counter-counter-counter-agents, the problem is no longer to identify the murderer, nor even to predict the outcome, but simply to follow what the devil is going on. It's not uncommon, at movies of this genre, to hear whispered arguments in the audience over who's on whose side, which desperado was or wasn't lurking in the corner of the frame at the railroad station, whether X is only *pretending* to go along with Y in hopes of something or other, and so on. Characters who appear to be passionately in love for half of the film turn out, not infrequently, to be only using each other for disparate ends. But we may later learn they've been on the same team after all. The hero goes through many changes (Who are his friends? Who are his enemies? For whom is he working?), and often these basic questions of plot remain unresolved even after the caper is clearly over. Such movies not only concern people who are busy putting each other on; their very texture is saturated with offhand lampooning of famous sequences from other films, of public figures, of political events, of homosexuality, of scientific gadgets, of cultural fads, and whatnot, as though, wrote Renata Adler in a review of one such thriller, "the creators had simply set out a fly-paper mood of irony and hoped that a lot of funny ideas about things would flutter in from all over and get stuck." Such creators seem hypersensitive to the feeling that life, qua metaphor of theatre, is a musical-thriller-comedy—sentimental, rough, satirical, melodramatic, impressionistic, realistic, and on and on. Obviously, then, no one theatrical convention embraces an adequate number of life's facets, and categories— drama, comedy, mystery—become inherently absurd.

The insight is not original with them; artists have always been plagued by this fundamental limitation. What *is* new is their refusal to embrace or even accept limitation, to work within it, to approach their material honestly, to *risk* appearing foolish. As their conviction is sapped, their courage fails, and then their integrity goes. Denying that art is limitation (Stravinsky has said, "The more art is limited, the more it is free"), their solution is to include as many categories as they can think of, and to immunize themselves against attack on the ground of falsehood by coming on tongue in cheek. When they seem to be making fun of themselves as well (a device Miss Adler has named "auto-spoof"), their work is very difficult to criticize. Like a pianist who hasn't the courage to practice hard and see how far he can go, they doodle around at the keyboard. It would be pointless to call attention to a missed note.

71

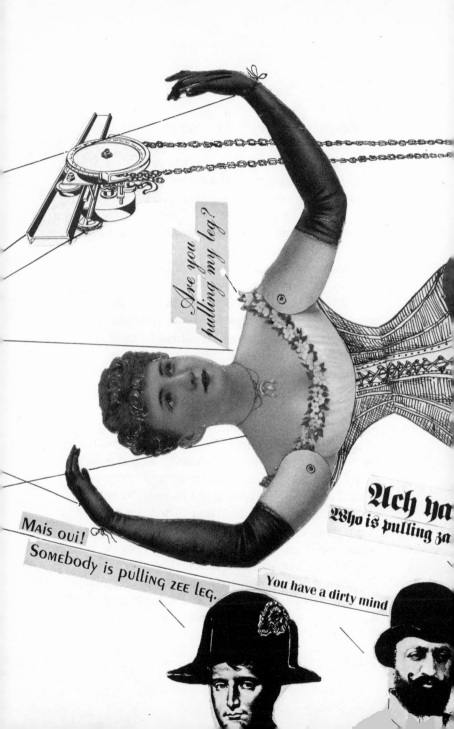

Spoof films train people to keep their cool, as do all put-ons. To put someone on is, almost by definition, to rob him of his cool. For, roughly speaking, loss of cool follows upon involvement of nearly any sort—especially upon involvement in an unworthy object, a hoax. The demands of intricate plotting, allusions to cinematic history, recognizable bits of satire, and other artifices help keep directors at a safe distance from the action of their films. Concomitantly, they never allow audiences to get caught up, either. Both creators and audience manage to avoid "blowing their cool." Their triumph of cool in the face of great excitement (both saw the silliness behind it) is at once paralleled and bolstered by the hero, for whom the retention of cool has become an altogether transcendent value. The hero demonstrates that one may remain uninvolved not only with experience one is depicting or beholding but with experience one is living as well. Whether James Bond is about to be seduced by a beauty queen or bisected by a laser beam, he remains as witty, as self-possessed, as detached—as *cool*—as a cocktail-party raconteur.

To be sure, the cool hero descends from a distinguished tradition in American culture, especially in cinema—from Gary Cooper's laconic Westerner to Humphrey Bogart's hard-boiled private eye, who retained their composure at either end of a gun. But the coolness of these old heroes was a tactic rather than an essence; we responded to it not as a mood of detachment that matched our own but as a kind of victory over danger. Because we were involved, because the filmmakers were involved, the climax of our aesthetic pleasure came when the heroes revealed that they were involved, too (revelation of his "humanity" practically became Bogart's trademark), and we learned, finally, that their coolness was only a front.

The highly successful film "Harper" is hardly one of the worst offenders in the omnispoof school—though its plot is sensationally confused, and Lauren Bacall is present to amplify the Camped-up echoes of the Humphrey Bogart-Sam Spade detective movies of the forties—but it does contain a remarkable interchange that may help to illustrate the dimensions of the cop-out. Pamela Tiffin asks Paul Newman (coolness itself) why he is on the caper, getting beat up, destroying his marriage, playing the private-eye game, and so on (the Existential questions—Who are you? Why are you you?—that any put-on must circumvent). Newman replies with a long, fast, impassioned gibberish patter: "As long as there are Communists in the Kremlin, criminals on the streets," etc., etc., "Lew Harper will be on the job!" Miss Tiffin is confused (our natural reaction). She asks, "*Are you putting me on?*" Newman lets out with his characteristic are-you-for-real laugh (the inevitable defense), somewhere between a guffaw and a Bronx cheer. End of conversation. But wait a minute. Has her question (vital and relevant) been answered, or only evaded? His laugh seems to mean "Of course I'm putting you on, you silly ass; I am playing this game for entirely *other* reasons." What are they? They don't exist. (The director unquestionably doesn't know what they are. Nor does the writer of the screenplay.) The point is that the gibberish constitutes his *real* reasons, expressed in terms that logically extend their absurdity. The *style* of his response, however, goes further than revealing insight through self-mockery. By couching revelation in the put-on, Harper denies its content, leaving an empty impression of mystery, escaping embarrassment at his own identity. He —along with the filmmakers—has used the put-on to cop out on the question.

From this interchange, we extrapolate: The whole movie is a put-on, a cop-out. Question: "How can you watch such stuff?" Answer: "Don't be pompous. You're being put on." Just as the private eye is embarrassed to own up to his identity, the thriller is embarrassed to admit it is a thriller. This cushions the audience's embarrassment at going to a thriller. Intellectuals, presumably, can only sit through a thriller with an attitude of overriding irony. Alfred Hitchcock was probably the first director to place *himself* at a slightly ironic distance from the action of his films; his own subtle mockery helped him confect high-gross thrillers that serious people might enjoy without losing their sense of superiority. Hollywood, which had so often been reprimanded for playing down to audiences, began to evolve a less noticed, more cynical trick—playing *up*. It allowed directors to wallow in undisciplined facetiousness—an attitude that jumbles self-deprecation and apology-in-advance with self-indulgence and disregard for the moral and technical problems posed by one's material. People who wouldn't be caught dead being moved or excited by a straight adventure story—even a good one—can be "amused" when offered an implicit wink from the filmmaker that signifies "We aren't taking this stuff any more seriously than you are."

How does "Harper" resolve its manifold complexities? After many false leads and twists, the murderer turns out to be Harper's best friend. We expect that one of them will surely kill the other in the last scene, but, instead, Harper turns wearily away from his friend's pointed gun and the film ends on a frozen closeup of him. His arms are outstretched in a gigantic shrug, as if to ask, "What did you expect out of life?" or, more pointedly, "What did you expect out of a movie? Out of art?"

The put-on is becoming a major communication option in intercourse between artist and critic, or, for that matter, between artist and society at large. This option has been, in some respects, overdue. Artists get asked a lot of stupid questions they don't feel like answering. Before the advent of the put-on, however, outright reluctance garnered an artist a reputation for surliness; playing along, on an interviewer's

own terms, made him appear shallow or inarticulate. "The Interview," a brilliant Ernest Pintoff-Mel Brooks animated cartoon of a few years back, epitomized this hangup. A Monk-type jazz musician, asked questions like "What does your piece express?," mumbled involuted hipster incoherencies: "You know, man, I start wailing, I'm into that groove, I listen to the other cats, I just *blow*—you dig, man?"

Recently, on a Channel 13 television broadcast, members of the Blues Project were asked this same question. Traditionally, musicians have prided themselves on their inability to talk with civilians. But, without hesitation, a member of the Project replied, "Man, this piece expresses what *every*body feels about *every*thing." Asked how the group got together, he replied, "We're *still* not together." (A classic put-on ploy: knowingly embracing a wrong but semantically plausible meaning—the chief bravura of John Lennon's prose.) When pressed, the Project member said they met as trolls in the Black Forest.

In another recent Channel 13 interview, the jazz bass player Charlie Mingus was asked by Dennis Azzarella (who seemed almost a parody of unhip ofay) whether a violent Harlem ballet, "Long Hot Summer," contained anti-white feeling.

"There weren't even any white people in it," Mingus replied. "I didn't see anything hostile, did you? Just a happy little Negro community beating each other up."

When pressed about the ballet's "message," Mingus said, "When I see *your* people dance, girls jumping around on the 'Ed Sullivan Show,' I can't see no messages."

"Are you putting me on?" Azzarella whined helplessly, glancing over at his cameraman.

Ernst von Salomon achieved a masterpiece through the form of interview put-on in his novel "Der Fragebogen," which he constructed as a detailed reply to a questionnaire that the Allies circulated in Germany as part of their de-Nazification program.

The interview, indeed, offers a prime matrix for the put-on. This may be a perverse rejection of the interview process as a social symbol. (So one enters schools, jobs, the Army, etc.) It is also, surely, a pragmatic response to the difficulty of questions in general. Honest answers are hard, because they can be disadvantageous (How much money are you entitled to deduct from your income tax?), because they are unknown (What do you believe?), or because they are boring (What have you been doing with yourself?). The put-on resolves all difficulties—it breaks up sets, disorients the interviewer, ridicules the interview process, communicates "real" ideas and feelings, yet deflates the seriousness of questions and replies. The now classic *Playboy* interview with Bob Dylan, by Nat Hentoff, must represent the apogee of this option. Hentoff deliberately "chose to play straight man in [my] questions, believing that to have done otherwise would have stemmed the freewheeling flow of Dylan's responses." Some excerpts from their dialogue may illustrate the complexity of put-on technique:

PLAYBOY: What about [your old fans'] charge that you vulgarized your natural gifts?

DYLAN: It's like going out to the desert and screaming, and then having little kids throw their sandbox at you. I'm only twenty-four. These people that said this— were they Americans?

PLAYBOY: What made you decide to go the rock-'n'-roll route?

DYLAN: Carelessness. I lost my one true love. I started drinking. The first thing I know, I'm in a card game. Then I'm in a crap game. I wake up in a pool hall. Then this big Mexican lady drags me off the table, takes me to Philadelphia. She leaves me alone in her house, and it burns down. I wind up in Phoenix. I get a job as a Chinaman. . . . Needless to say, he burned the house down and I hit the road. The first guy that picked me up asked me if I wanted to be a star. What could I say?

PLAYBOY: And that's how you became a rock-'n'-roll singer?

DYLAN: No, that's how I got tuberculosis.

PLAYBOY: Let's turn the question around: Why have you stopped composing and singing protest songs?

DYLAN: The word "protest," I think, was made up for people undergoing surgery. It's an amusement-park word. A normal person in his righteous mind would have to have the hiccups to pronounce it honestly. The word "message" strikes me as having a hernia-like sound. It's just like the word "delicious." Also the word "marvellous." You know, the English can say "marvellous" pretty good. They can't say "raunchy" so good, though. Well, we each have our thing.

PLAYBOY: Can't you be a bit more informative?

DYLAN: Nope.

PLAYBOY: How do you get your kicks these days?

DYLAN: I hire people to look into my eyes, and then I have them kick me.

PLAYBOY: And that's the way you get your kicks?

DYLAN: No. Then I *forgive* them; that's where my kicks come in.

PLAYBOY: Did you ever have the standard boyhood dream of growing up to be President?

85

DYLAN: No. When I was a boy, Harry Truman was President. Who'd want to be Harry Truman?

PLAYBOY: Well, let's suppose that you *were* the President. What would you accomplish during your first thousand days?

DYLAN: Well, just for laughs, so long as you insist, the first thing I'd do is probably move the White House. Instead of being in Texas, it'd be on the East Side in New York. McGeorge Bundy would definitely have to change his name, and General McNamara would be forced to wear a coonskin cap and shades.

In conversation, the put-on nearly always arises in response to questions. When the questioner and questionee represent opposing philosophies, invocation of the put-on precludes any possible agreement. Even though it's really a defensive weapon, the put-on almost always provides an offensive for the questionee, representative of the smaller, more helpless faction, making his group appear In and the larger, more powerful group of the questioner appear Out. Because the put-on is a close-range weapon, it is usually, by a curious mechanism, employed against the most sympathetic elements among the enemy. One might almost say that it is invoked when the moment of reconciliation is in sight, at the point when dialogue might begin —to prevent dialogue, to guarantee continued estrangement, and to protect the integrity of a beleaguered minority position. Thus, a bohemian delinquent will usually treat policemen with careful deference, but he will mercilessly put on a friendly probation officer or social worker. An artist will put on a dumb but eager fan who inquires about his creative methods but not a total boor who evinces no interest in art whatever. By the same token, Negroes commonly put on white liberals. As an exception, Stokely Carmichael built up a nearly legendary reputation in S.N.C.C. by putting on Southern bigots (subtly sassing Lowndes County deputies, mimicking their swaggers, addressing them in Yiddish)—an almost unheard-of practice. He could get away with it simply because the form of the put-on is so elusive; the victim is never sure precisely what's happening. In this manner, the put-on brings the submerged antagonisms of a relationship perilously close to the surface—*without actually allowing them to come into the open*. If the victim chooses to notice the put-on, the perpetrator can always feign absolute innocence. A put-on may even be veiled in expressions of injured purity:

A: What are you trying to do—make fun of me, nigger?

B: Oh *no,* suh. No *suh,* Boss.

In less explosive situations, this impalpable quality prevents forthright discussion of the resentments that may have produced the put-on in the first place:

A: Why are you treating me contemptuously?

B: Contemptuously? That's just a hostile projection. What ever are you talking about? You must be paranoid.

A: Well, perhaps I am oversensitive. Perhaps I'm imagining things.

The victim is often at least a partially willing victim; a bewildered guilt makes him reluctant to press the issue. But his vague feeling of having been placed at an unfair disadvantage, of having been ridiculed, persists semiconsciously. He may subsequently take indirect revenge.

Although there may be as many variations as practitioners, the extended in-group put-on usually improvises on two classic formats:

(1) Relentless Agreement: The perpetrator beats his victim to every low cliché the latter might possibly mouth.

(2) Actualization of the Stereotype: The perpetrator *personifies* every cliché about his group, realizes his adversary's every negative expectation. He becomes a grotesque rendition of his presumed identity, faking heated emotion.

Either of these options—caricaturing the victim or caricaturing the victim's image of oneself —is called into play when an out-group representative attempts to engage an in-group representative on the subject of their estrangement. The second option, being more *obviously* hostile, is more often taken at face value by the victim, but both options serve to affirm the belief that communication between disparate worlds is impossible—to affirm in-group solidarity and isolation. Both types grow progressively more extravagant. Here are some examples:

I. Young vs. Old: A well-disposed but bewildered adult tries to talk with a "rebellious adolescent" about generational gap. The young man responds:

(1) "Ah, I don't know. . . . Kids today —they're always running. But who knows where they're going? Crazy clothes, loud music—if you wanna call it music—fast cars, drinking, smoking, drugs. The next thing you know, we'll be going out with girls."

(2) "Why don't you go play with your mutual funds or something? Why don't you get off my back? I just want to bug out on your nowhere scene, nowhere man. Excuse me, I gotta go dig some groovy sounds and sniff a pot of airplane glue. Lemme peel out on my boss Harley; that mother takes off like a big-assed bird."

II. Black vs. White: A benevolent progressive tries to express his questioning support of civil rights. The militant Negro responds:

(1) "You're two hundred per cent right. I mean, with freedom goes responsibility. You can't just grab everything right off. Some demonstrations can only hurt our cause, you know what I mean? Like Dr. King says, our people've got to meet body force with Soul Force. He sets a good example. Like Joe Louis. He was a helluva fighter, huh? But he knew his place. Now, a man like Adam Clayton Powell, he's overstepping his bounds. He takes advantage. Ralph Bunche. That was a good nigger. 'Cept he couldn't sing and dance. What do you think?"

(2) "Don't make your superego gig with me, ofay baby. Your granddaddy rape my

91

grandmammy, and now you tell me doan screw your daughter? Well, beat up side my black head and whup my humble black butt, but don't offer me none of the *su*preme delectafactotory blessings of equalorama, 'cause when this bitch blows you gonna feel black man's machete in the soft flesh of your body, dig?"

III. Dove vs. Hawk: A patriotic Republican tries to start a serious conversation on the Southeast Asian situation. The subversive responds:

(1) "Absolutely. We're just making the same mistake we made in Korea, pussyfooting in those jungle swamps like gorillas. Our country's going to lose its first war unless we go on up North and nuke 'em and nape 'em. That's the only language those Commies understand, those Red butchers. We should throw all our pinko bleeding-heart draft-card burners in jail, or ship 'em over to Ho Chi Minh, where they belong."

(2) "Sure, I'd just love to go into the military myself, start a little education program of my own. Maybe take a squadron out to defoliate Central Park and burn down Rockefeller Center. Give you imperialist warmongers and your Texas Führer in the White House something to think about."

IV. Hip vs. Square: A Sunday Villager from uptown seeks illumination on the bohemian mystique. The hippie responds:

(1) "Yeah, well, you know if we could

get jobs we'd lap 'em up, but who'd hire us, man? Like we're *dirty*. I haven't had a bath since last February. And you should see the chick that shares my pad—freaky little mind-blower. You really got the life, Charlie—kids, a couple parakeets, a beer and a ball game. You don't worry about nothin', hear? You're on the right track. Listen, could you spare a quarter? I haven't had breakfast."

(2) Sullen silence interspersed with incoherent grunts. Hippie finally grins sardonically and offers the square a reefer. "Somethin' is happening here, but you don't know what it is. *Do* you, Mistah Jones?"

V. Homosexual vs. Heterosexual: A straight (another meaning of this protean word) but enlightened man, evincing his enlightenment, seeks data. The homosexual responds:

(1) "Why, of *course* it's a *sickness,* there's no *question*. Take me. My father was *weak, hen*pecked. It's psychological. My mother wouldn't let me wear long *pants* till I was fourteen. And then the *Ar*my. Well, *you* know. It's better than *an*imals. My analyst thinks I'm progressing toward a real ad*just*ment."

(2) Mock flirtation; strokes the victim, bats eyelashes, dentalizes or lisps. "You sure know how to dress. And you're so under*standing*. Why don't you loosen up a little, Mary?"

Robert Hoebermann

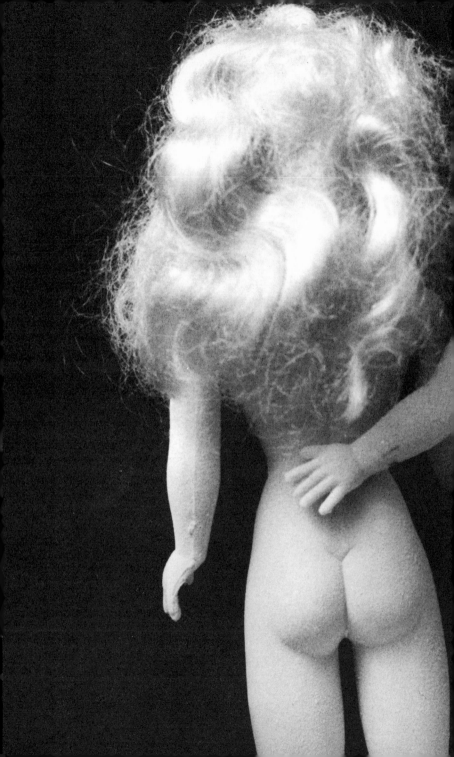

Robert Hoebermann

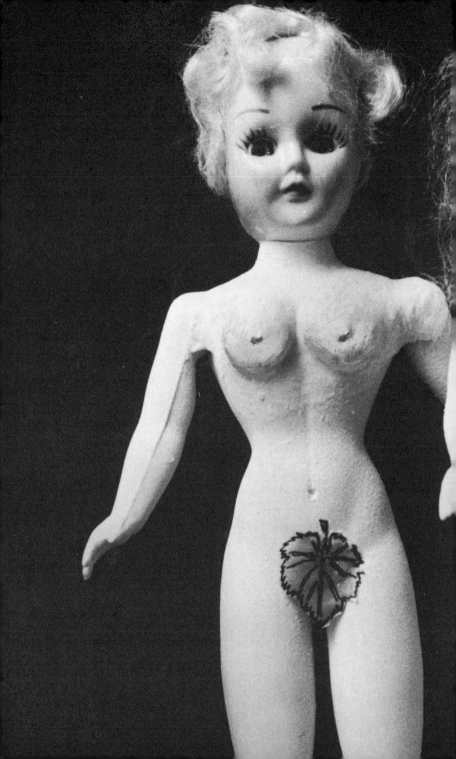

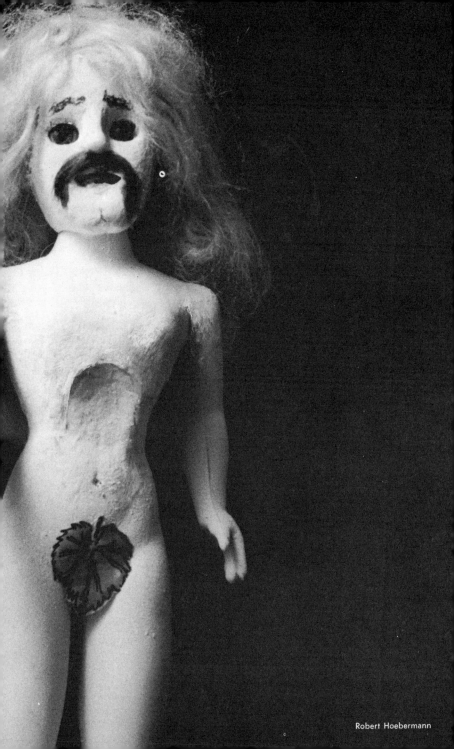

Robert Hoebermann

In less threatening situations, the put-on itself can become the basis of the come-on. Such cases prostitute the form: genuine transaction is avoided (cop-out), but time passes and nothing real or interesting happens. Asked about his background at a party, a young man replies in a Westbrook Van Vorhis voice, "I was born of rich but humble parents in a little mining town called Juarez. . . ." There is no promise of engagement in what is to come, because there is no potential for fake-out. Is the truth so boring or embarrassing? This species of ersatz put-on lacks the element of tension. It is, at bottom, only a "bit," and occurs when the put-on itself becomes an established set—when a person begins actually to put himself on, and can no longer betray *any* straight feelings. Once the put-on is explicitly labelled (as by a new comedian, who titled his first record album "Take-Offs and Put-Ons"), uncertainty dissolves and old-fashioned kidding takes over.

Like sentimentality, the put-on offers a lazy man's substitute for feeling as well as for thought. Again, the form contains a built-in escape clause.

People are not so much unsure of their feelings as unsure what feeling may be appropriate. Thus, a trite expression of feeling now has the advantage of being equivocal.

"How did you like the play?"

"Very moving."

Perfect, take it how you will. Whether the play was moving, corny, or itself a put-on, the question has been answered—assuming a slightly ambiguous intonation—appropriately.

A related but more calculated and aggressive dodge involves, quite simply, replying in gibberish when no honest response springs to mind.

"How did you like the play?"

"It was over the bush, man."

This sort of remark is seldom challenged. On the rare occasion when a victim asks, "What does 'over the bush' mean?," the perpetrator assumes a vaguely irritated tone and replies, "You know, man, it's like funk, only trippier," or some such nonsense. It takes a hardy victim to press the matter further.

Another subtle, and eventually devastating, ploy might be called the "silent put-on." Its perpetrator sits in rapt attention—nodding vigorously, asking occasional questions—as his victim pontificates. Gradually, the victim begins to suspect, rightly or wrongly, that his silent audience knows a good deal more about the subject at hand than he's letting on ("Here I've been running on about modern art on the basis of catalogue blurbs, and this fellow is obviously an important critic or painter himself"). As the perpetrator begins to reinforce this suspicion with improbable expressions of awe, the victim dimly perceives that, having been given enough rope to hang himself, he has behaved like a pompous, ignorant ass. Typically, he tapers off in embarrassment and excuses himself.

Not all conversational put-ons are so viciously intended. Some, particularly those employed by people who are either high on mind-affecting chemicals or have experimented considerably with such drugs, are simply a form of exploratory play—the interpersonal equivalent of set-breaking put-ons in serious art. LSD and, to a lesser extent, marijuana and hashish continuously dissolve and re-form the structure of reality, until being put through changes—and following these changes wherever they may lead—constitutes the drug user's most real and pleasurable sort of experience. The word "straight," therefore, denotes both not going through changes (not appreciating put-ons) and not being under the influence of drugs. Hallucinogens subject one's world of static reality (the Comprehensive Come-On) to constant fake-outs—transform it, indeed, into a gigantic put-on. The psychedelic solution to this flux: embrace every tangent, every fake-out with the same zeal. A conversational digression, perhaps initiated by a pun or misunderstanding, becomes altogether as important as the "main" conversation, and may supersede it entirely. When "heads" relate to one another, they perpetually put each other through changes, bust up each other's sets before sets can solidify. Flowing downstream with these changes is, for these people, serious fun. When heads relate to straight people, however, this set-breaking activity is experienced as put-on. A head's deliberately inappropriate behavior at a party—ranting, or talking nonsense, or demonstrating disproportionate affection toward strangers, or radically shifting the mood and emotional intensity of discourse— subjects his victims to a kind of involuntary "acid test." Either they are able to follow him through his changes—neutralizing and appreciating them with their own consciousnesses—or they persist in their straightness and are "freaked;" i.e., respond, by leaving or fighting, as if they were under attack. If they do the first, they are said to have been turned on; if the second, they can have quite a bad time. Hence the positive or negative reactions on the part of reporters interviewing creative performers who have been influenced by mind-bending drugs. A non-psychedelic illustration of the same principle turns up in "Don't Look Back," D. A. Pennebaker's *cinéma-vérité* movie of Dylan's London tour, a prolonged documentary of Dylan putting on the British—or, rather, putting them through changes. Some get turned on, some completely fail to perceive what's happening, and many get freaked.

Heads try to break up sets without malevolence, but their put-ons are sometimes so extreme that straight people mistake them for "scoring"—the sort of derision that Negroes call "signifying" and adolescents call "chopping," "ranking," or "sounding." Non-heads also may employ the put-on without malice. Sometimes understated facetiousness seems the only way to keep the ball rolling in a conversation that would be otherwise devoid of interest and amusement. When such put-ons pass unrecognized over the heads of one's companions, all parties can enjoy the proceedings on different levels and no feelings are ruffled.

In depicting put-on artists on the stage, Harold Pinter has shown how different their effects may be. Mick, in "The Caretaker," puts Davies through such cruel and violent changes that the old man becomes completely unhinged. Lenny, in "The Homecoming," enrages his father with his constant put-ons—but his terrible teasing goes unperceived by the other characters in the play. The audience therefore appreciates Lenny's every remark (he never says a straight word) on one plane while the other characters receive them on another. "He's always been my favorite brother, old Teddy," he tells Teddy's wife. "And, my goodness, we are proud of him here, I can tell you. Doctor of Philosophy and all that . . . leaves quite an impression. Of course, he's a very sensitive man, isn't he? Ted. Very. I've often wished I was as sensitive as he is." What the sister-in-law understands and what the audience understands are worlds apart in feeling.

The embarrassment at one's own predicament or identity which produces theatrical tongue-in-cheek (spoof) and conversational tongue-in-cheek (put-on) issues from an intermediate level of awareness—an awareness that reveals the inadequacy of a come-on but fails to suggest any useful alternative. The put-on, then, arises out of a *partial consciousness* of one's own ridiculousness, in the absence of sufficient courage or intellectual perseverance to see that ridiculousness through to its roots and to alter it.

At a large New York advertising agency, communication through hackneyed Madison Avenue-ese has become a source of embarrassment. Certain executives—usually the oldest and highest-ranking—will use a chestnut unself-consciously; e.g., "Why don't we put it out on the back stoop and see if the cat licks it up?" Others employ such expressions only reluctantly, making it clear that they know a trite saying when they use one: "Why don't we put it out on the back stoop and see if the cat licks it up, as the cliché goes." Yet the phrase "as the cliché goes" has achieved such currency around the agency that a third echelon, of junior executives, has come to recognize *it* as a cliché. Still too lazy or unimaginative to break away into a fresh image, they simply incorporate this further self-consciousness: "Why don't we put it out on the back stoop and see if the cat licks it up, as the cliché goes, as the cliché goes." This last solution is already close to a put-on, for it deals with embarrassment aggressively, ridiculing both the asininity of the top executives and the primitive self-consciousness of the secondary executives. The most "sophisticated" elements of the third group deal in outright put-ons; that is, they utter the unadorned cliché in precisely the same words as the top executives but in a way that suggests a transcendent awareness of its rich meaning or absurdity. Their intonation, gestures, or exaggerated emphases give notice that they are absolutely detached from the actual words, that their real intention is sarcastic, paradoxical, ironic, supportive, or, for that matter, whatever a superior may choose to think it is. (Young men at the agency who habitually express their ideas in this ambiguous mode are considered either especially gifted or subversive and dangerous. Their presence increases the general self-consciousness at conferences, and occasionally forces even some of the older executives into adopting a put-on style.)

A similar breeding pattern for the put-on, as an outgrowth of halfway consciousness, has occurred in advertising proper over the last fifteen years. Parodists, like Harvey Kurtzman's early *Mad* magazine and its imitators, and Jean Shepherd on the radio, helped to promote a growing self-consciousness among purveyors of the hard sell. The precocious soft-sell ads—not the more recent Doyle Dane Bernbach highly polished genre but the initial Bob Elliott and Ray Goulding Piel Bros. Harry-and-Bert campaign (later echoed, for another beer company, by Mike Nichols and Elaine May), or the Chevron campaign ("Chevron Supreme Fits Any Shape Gas Tank!," "With Chevron Supreme Gasoline Your Car Can Go Forwards and Backwards!," "When Your Car Runs Out of Chevron Supreme Gasoline It Will . . . Stop!")—formed a transitional phase to the reincarnation of hard sell in put-on guise.

Humorous soft sell underminded a tradition of advertisements that had a content, a reasonably logical, reasonably structured pitch for a product. Instead, it seemed to indicate that sales might result simply from (1) mention of the product, and (2) a laugh, derived somehow—anyhow—in connection with that mention. (When people began quoting tongue-in-cheek ads, their talk meant more sales as surely as a catchy jingle semiconsciously whistled.) Funny soft sell also seemed to attack the spinal cord of advertising, which is making claims for the product. It made fun of the very idea of making claims, especially exaggerated ones, and, along the way, of most other hard-sell techniques—endorsements, contests, giveaways, coupons.

Before long, hard sell ("coming on strong")

tried to incorporate some of the sense of ridiculousness that went into *Mad*-type parodies, and a good deal of the tongue-in-cheek that went into the soft sells of the middle fifties. What resulted was a species of super-hard sell that, figuratively, appends a sophisticated "as the cliché goes" after the cliché. For example, a bathetic fake-out in the final instant of a commercial makes the whole commercial look silly: An announcer seriously praises a brand of pork-and-beans, holding up two cans as he concludes his spiel. He claps the cans together for emphasis and catches his nose between them. Inevitably, some commercials simply use intonation or sheer exaggeration to let *us* know that *they* know better. They become an unspecific but roaring burlesque of themselves and of all advertising, thereby rising, or sinking, to the realm of nearly pure put-on.

The most common tenor for such advertising is super-frenzy or super-ecstasy. Where straight hard sell communicated sincere, if slightly incredible, enthusiasm for the product, put-on hard sell does cartwheels of shrieking exultation. Old TV hard sell for a beauty product might have had a Ted Mack or Arthur Godfrey look earnestly into the camera and say, "Believe me, girls —this stuff really works." A commercial for the same product might now picture a dowdy secretary converted in no time into a man-eating vamp. After a few over-a-bare-shoulder, feline growls, she says, "Buhlieve you *me,* gurrls—*this* stuff *rrrrrrhheeeelly* works." Clearly, a joke is intended; never was a secretary so draggletailed nor a temptress so seductive. The transformation seems preposterous—an iteration of Jules Feiffer's "Passionella." Yet the hyperbole cannot have ironic purposes; surely we are expected to come away believing that the beauty product does indeed work. Perhaps not as well as in the dramatization? Then, how well?

In a ten-second television spot, a couple find a certain brand of coffee in the supermarket and fall all over each other in hysterical joy. Possibly we are meant to feel that the advertising agency has joined with us in a humorous conspiracy against the sponsor—that we are somehow in on the same joke, and meant to buy the product anyhow, perhaps in gratitude for having been entertained and flattered. (The advertising put-on contains an implicit presumption that straight hard sell insulted our intelligence.)

Just as a person can get away with saying something stupid (cop-out) by effusing peripheral clues that indicate he *knows* what he's saying is stupid (indeed, that imply he might say something smart if he chose to), so can an advertisement now get away with being hard sell and at the same time cop out on hard sell's fundamental responsibility—to explain just how good the product is. The put-on, in the first case, provides a stupid statement with the same apparent value as a smart statement; in the second case, it renders an impossibly vague, impossibly hyperbolic claim as valuable (to the sponsor) as a precise one.

Put-on hyperbole (hyperbole, that is, which is to be taken seriously but not *that* seriously) typically clothes itself in magical or fantastic garb. Thus, among cleansing products potency is represented—not in simile but in metaphor so immediately visual as to seem close to documentary—by armored knights charging on horseback, their whitening lances aimed at small children; by full-scale tornadoes; by meddlesome birds who fly in kitchen windows; by anti-dirt bombs dropped from fighter planes to score direct, highly explosive hits on soiled linen; by transparent shields that jet visitors at six-inch altitudes across scuffproof floors; by washing machines that, seconds after the product is administered, swell to three times their normal height, dwarfing the housewife; by Irish, Mary Poppins-ish maids sailing in from the blue, depositing their wonderworking suds, and soaring off again, singing a jingle; and by a detergent that zooms you out of the kitchen as though your sink were a launching pad. Toward the conclusion of each dramatization, the housewife praises the detergent godsend in a paroxysm of commingled surprise and delight that would seem disproportionate had she just

112

been informed of her husband's election to high office.

Had a sample of such frenzied hyperbole been offered fifteen years ago, in the time of earnest hard sell, viewers would have found themselves bewildered at an apparently insane joke. Hyperbole in humor has traditionally served as a device for satire or irony. Advertising, however, uses humorous hyperbole in a new and confusing way—deliberately trafficking in ambiguity to obscure the crucial questions for the consumer: What does the product accomplish, and why is it better than the competition?

Robert Hoebermann

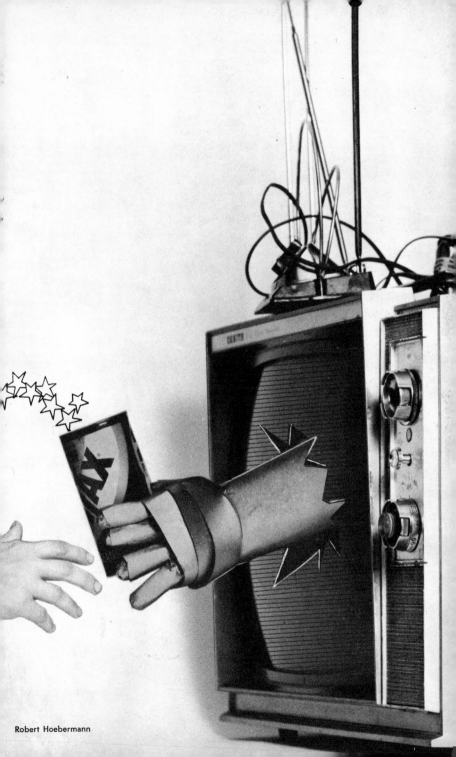

Robert Hoebermann

Robert Hoebermann

Yet advertising is hardly the only form to use hyperbole whose relation to truth is confoundingly unclear. Similar obfuscation caused certain critics trouble when they tried to get at "MacBird." Finding it unfunny, they were instructed to look for political allegory; finding it impossibly farfetched, they were instructed to appreciate farce. This kind of hyperbole implies that we have been moved in the proper direction of truth—but some indeterminate distance beyond truth. We may or may not take it all seriously, but we may not hold the author accountable for our choice. An implied self-mockery claims the jump on mocking attempts from the outside. Tom Wolfe has, thus far, most fully realized these hyperbolic techniques in journalism.

Put-on excess garnered an audience for the 007 books which would have been embarrassed to read Mickey Spillane, who was no less hyperbolic in a straight way. Fleming's names—Miss Moneypenny, Odd Job, Tiffany Case, Pussy Galore, Kissy Suzuki—might have sprung from "V" or "Catch-22." Literary parodies of his series—

120

and there were a number—tended to flop; they only exaggerated an exaggeration and were scarcely distinguishable from the original. With each James Bond movie, the self-mocking hyperbole became increasingly pronounced fairly poking the viewer in the ribs, until, finally, "Casino Royale" was no more than a frenetic comic romp, devoid of thriller pretensions. Bond initiated a cinematic form, and then became the only possible parody of it himself—a sort of manufactured Camp. From revivals of the old "Batman" serials it was a short step to the fabrication of a TV series, the resuscitation of "The Green Hornet," and the invention of "Captain Nice" and "Mr. Terrific." More Campsters are waiting in the wings.

If people enjoy laughing at hyperbolic work that's intended seriously (Camp), the argument seems to go, why not confect "serious" work for them to laugh at (put-on)? This oddly marketable type of comedy—the earnest presentation of art that is so bad or so ridiculous that the public will pay to snigger at it—isn't altogether unprecedented. The Cherry Sisters, a hopelessly inadequate singing duo of the early nineteen-hundreds, were booked into theatres where customers came to hiss, laugh, and throw vegetables at them. Nobody ever knew for sure whether they realized they were terrible or not. Around 1920, George M. Cohan wrote "The Tavern," a melodrama that was directed and played for laughs, and again nobody knew whether it was written straight or as an intentional satire of melodrama.

Today, manufactured Camp is becoming an entertainment industry. The dramatic clichés of a generation ago—from "The natives are restless tonight" to "What did you say that masked man's name was?" to "How do things look, Doc?"—are suddenly coming back in droves, funny this time around. Invited to a "pig party," college boys ask the ugliest girls they can find and let them, as the evening wears on, discover the cruel principle of the soirée by induction. Capitol Records recently put out three successful albums featuring the off-key warbling of a talentless California grandmother named Elva Miller, who had always aspired to be a songstress. Mrs. Miller sang a few of her "greatest hits" with lush orchestral accompaniment on the "Ed Sullivan Show." The Fugs ascended to stardom when their sound was more awful than a roomful of drunken teamsters. (In the past year, their musicianship has improved; they've compensated by pushing their unconventional personalities further in the direction of the far-out.) Freddie and the Dreamers seemed to realize that their charm lay in their simpleminded badness, and who knows what to make of the New Vaudeville Band, a collection of Mod Rudy Vallées?

Artists may construct extreme personalities for themselves, which compete with their work for public attention. The put-on personality may be largely confected (as with Salvador Dali or Phyllis Diller or Monti Rock III) or an extension of actual traits (as with Brother Theodore or Gypsy Boots or the Rolling Stones). Celebrities may, after they are established, send up their legitimate selves. Many modern performers seem prepared to deliberately caricature what they once were or were expected to be. In an earlier era, John Barrymore and Mae West did something of the same thing. Bogart, Robert Morley, and Peter Lorre all did it in "Beat the Devil," in 1954. But their self-mockery was diaphanous compared to the jobs directors have had other stars do on themselves: Burt Lancaster in "The Crimson Pirate," James Cagney in "One, Two, Three," Joan Crawford and Bette Davis in "What Ever Happened to Baby Jane?," Marilyn Monroe in "The Seven Year Itch," Jayne Mansfield in "Will Success Spoil Rock Hunter?," Anita Ekberg in "La Dolce Vita," Frank Sinatra and friends in "Ocean's 11," Jeanne Moreau and Brigitte Bardot in "Viva Maria," and half a dozen French celebrities in Godard cameo roles. Do the actors fully realize how they are burlesquing themselves? What is being made fun of? The star? Or the public's image of the star?

remember being on both sides of put-ons circa junior high school, although we didn't use the word back then. An interchange would go something like this:

A: My grandmother died today.

B: Gee, I'm sorry to hear that. How old was she?

A: Ninety-three.

B: Gee, that's pretty old.

A: Yeah. Well, at least they saved the baby.

B: Gee, she must've had a good doctor.

Dialogues like this could go on for quite a while, given sufficient gullibility on the part of B. (They were always better with an audience.) An artful put-on elicited some genuine response to a phony statement. No one was wholly immune to the form; the initial essence of the put-on was plausible—it simply grew more farfetched as it went along. The trick was to catch on quick. If you did, you could laugh with the other guys, although any response, once you'd been hooked, left you looking foolish. If you didn't, you were a dead man.

Adolescent put-ons illustrate the intimate relationship between the put-on and the put-down. The put-down is an insult with imagination—a form that, at its best, leaves the offended party muttering, "Wonder what he meant by that." "Are you putting me down?" is asked nearly as often as "Are you putting me on?" The reason for this affinity may be partly that the put-on is a basically hostile means of expression (in a speaker, hostile to his own feelings and to his antagonist; in an artist, hostile to his materials, his audience, and his own talent) and partly that insult devoid of cleverness is no longer tolerated. The fanciful element that has refined the put-down is the put-on. (N.B.C. recently presented a gala resuscitation of the old "Colgate Comedy Hour" that featured "new trends in comedy, including the put-on and the put-down.") Much of Lenny Bruce's material was based on this conjunction. It is currently apotheosized in such so-called "insult comics" as Don Rickles. For years, Mort Sahl has come onstage carrying a newspaper. He reads a headline—say, " 'Johnson Denies Mining Rivers and Shelling the North Is Escalation of War, Calls Moves "Military Steps Toward Peace." ' " Before Sahl has even taken off from it, the audience responds to the tacit understanding that the *news itself* is a put-on—doublethink that scarcely requires parody.

'War.

ake love.

Peace

Make war.

It may be that some element of the put-on has always resided at the base of art—what E. M. Forster called "shamming"—but it has taken the contemporary sensibility to discern and articulate these latent elements, to turn facetiousness into a full aesthetic, or even moral, category. It may be that the put-on offers the only remaining possibility for aesthetic or philosophical synthesis in a world that has become staggeringly confused and grotesque. It may be that when reality becomes too complex to master, the best we can do is adopt an attitude toward it. T. S. Eliot wrote that Pope, Dryden, and Swift showed how contempt, resentment, and disgust might be forms for genius. Perhaps our own self-conscious century—with its artists trying to transcend the limits of language, to redefine their media, to find the least uncomfortable view of their own lives—will, in time, produce the Put-On Genius. Unhappily, audiences that can't take any art straight with confidence will have paid a high price in the waiting, and may have a hard time recognizing him when he arrives.

A generation is coming of age in America that doesn't take the news straight, that doesn't take the utterances of public figures straight, that doesn't take social games straight. It suspects not only art but the whole range of modern experience. It sees giant con games everywhere. It sees "the system" itself as a con game. Parodoxically, this generation—so obsessed with the themes of falsehood, phoniness, and hypocrisy—has developed and refined the art of the put-on, as if driven to illustrate that what passes for "truth" and "reality" is often cruelly deceptive.

A complex society depends for its survival on some degree of mutual trust among its citizens. But a generation of Americans, having lost all patience with the dishonesties that lubricate social transactions, now appears ready to propagate its own distrust throughout society, to foist upon communication the very cancer it has protested against. The put-on may be a destructive device born out of desperation—a weapon to force people out, through confusion and loss of confidence, toward honesty. Perhaps a hope exists, however dubious, that the debasement of discourse will soon become intolerable—a hope that people, when their legs have been pulled almost to the breaking point, will at last begin to kick.